20 Easy Christmas Carols For Beginners Clarinet Book 2

Big Note Sheet Music With Lettered Noteheads

Michael Shaw

Copyright © 2016 Michael Shaw. All rights reserved. Including the right to reproduce this book or portions thereof, in any form. No part of this text may be reproduced in any form without the express written permission of the author.

Music Arrangements. All Christmas Carol arrangements in this book by **Michael Shaw Copyright © 2016**

ISBN: 1539099806
ISBN-13: 978-1539099802

www.mikesmusicroom.co.uk

Contents

We Wish You A Merry Christmas	1
Silent Night	4
Gather Around The Christmas Tree	6
Once In Royal David's City	8
Jingle Bells	10
While Shepherds Watched Their Flocks	14
Good Christian Men Rejoice	16
We Three Kings	18
Angels We Have Heard On High	22
Go Tell It On The Mountain	24
Angels From The Realms Of Glory	27
It Came Upon The Midnight Clear	28
Coventry Carol	31
Joy To The World	32
Christians Awake Salute The Happy Morn	34
Good King Wenceslas	36
Come, All Ye Shepherds	38
What Child Is This?	40
The Holly And The Ivy	42
I Heard The Bells On Christmas Day	44
About The Author	46

We Wish You A Merry Christmas

Traditional

♩ = 130

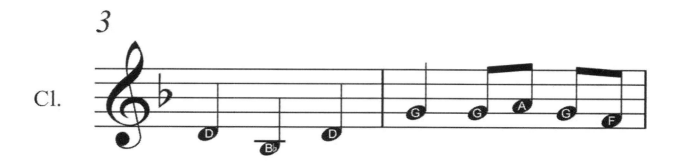

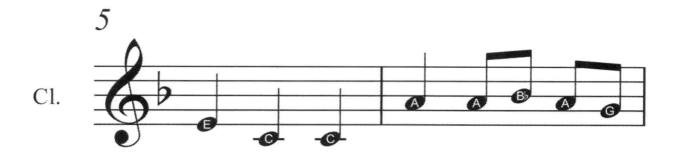

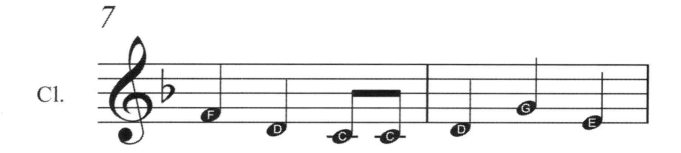

9

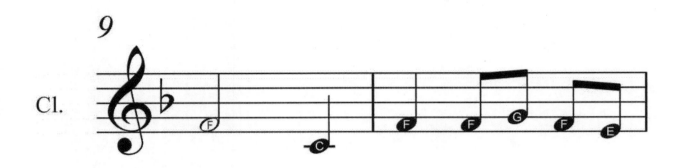

11

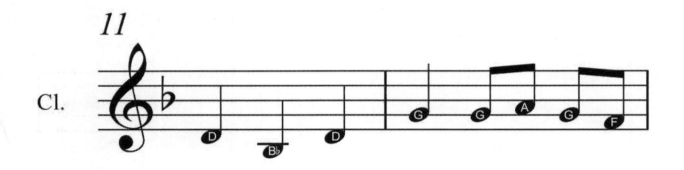

13

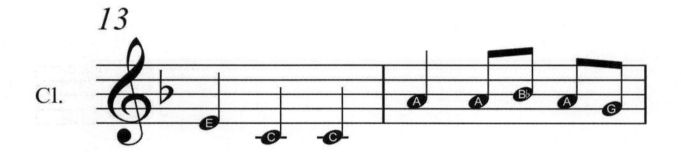

15

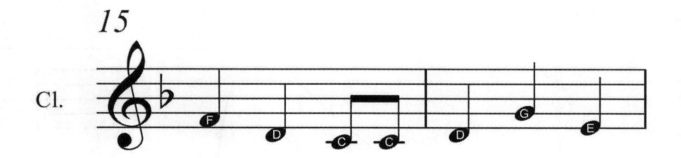

17

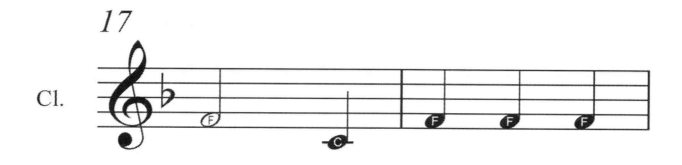

19

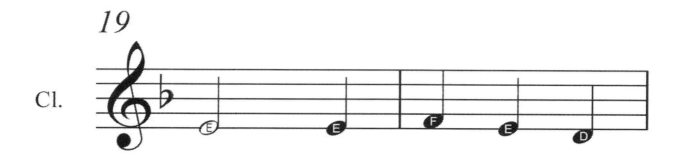

21

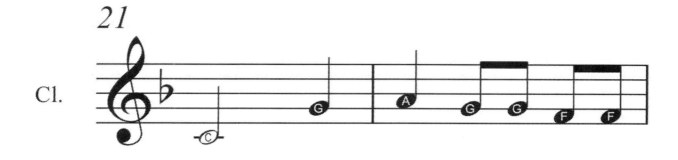

23

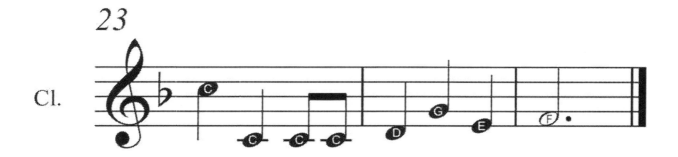

Silent Night

Traditional

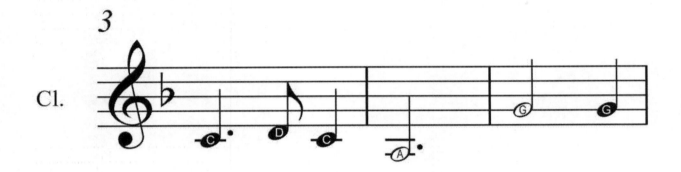

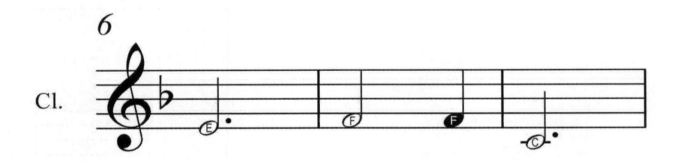

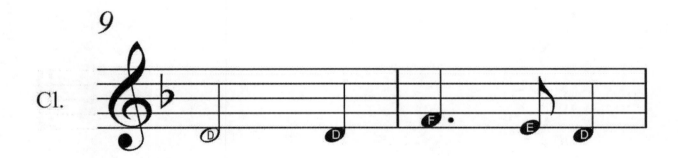

Gather Around The Christmas Tree

9

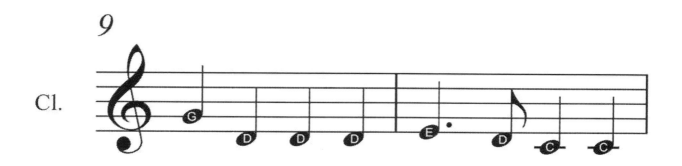

11

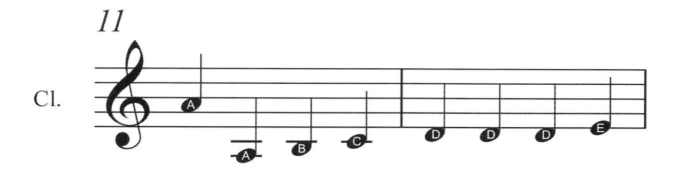

13

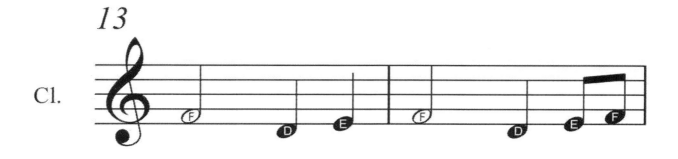

15

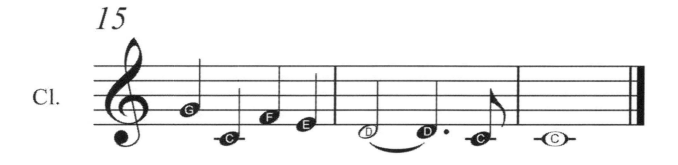

Once In Royal David's City

Henry John Gauntlett

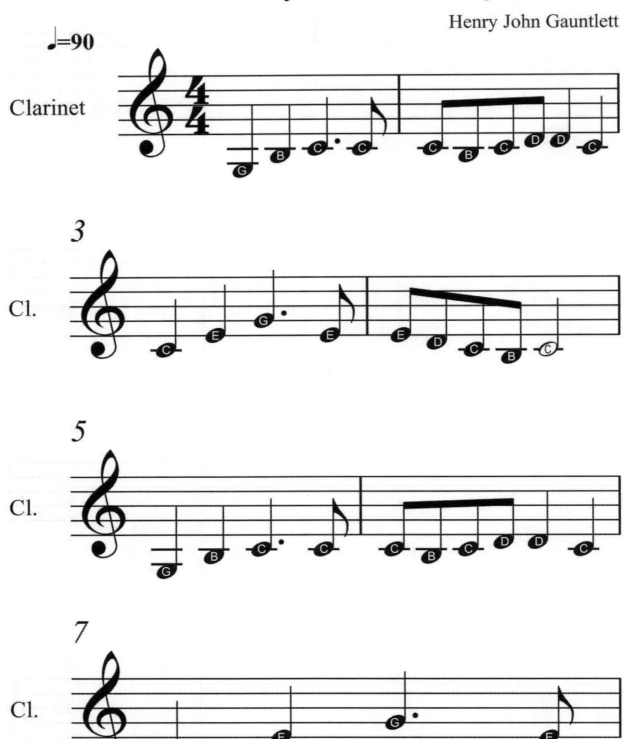

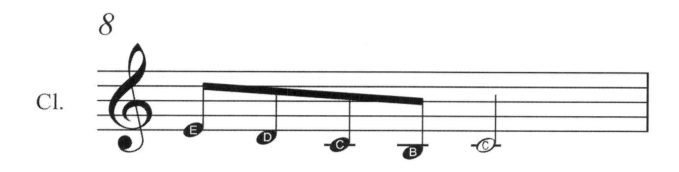

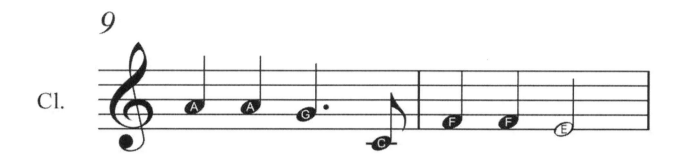

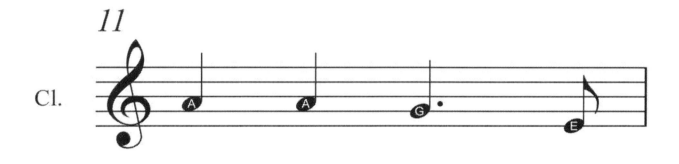

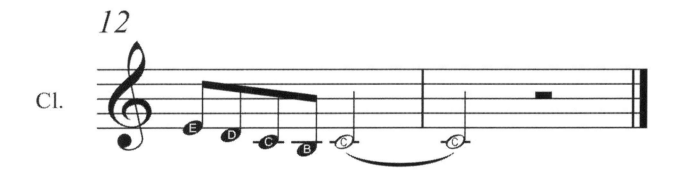

Jingle Bells

James Pierpoint

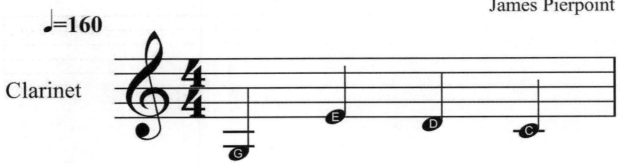
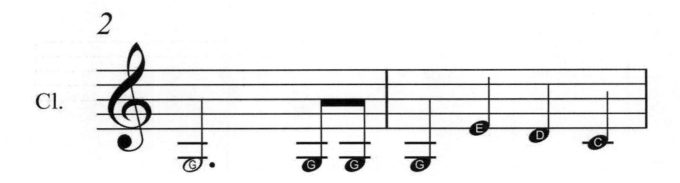
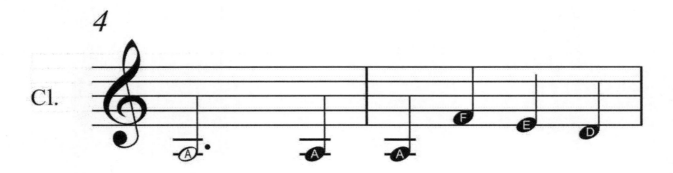

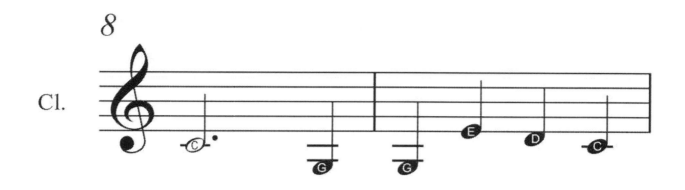

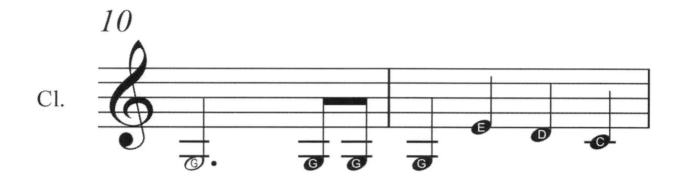

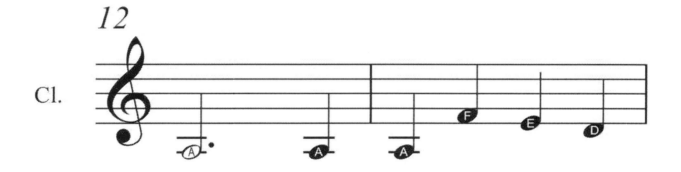

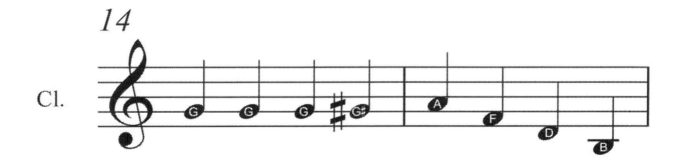

16
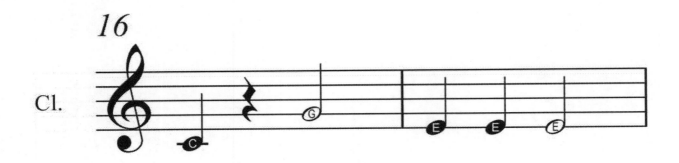

18
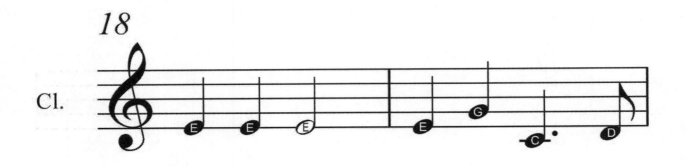

20
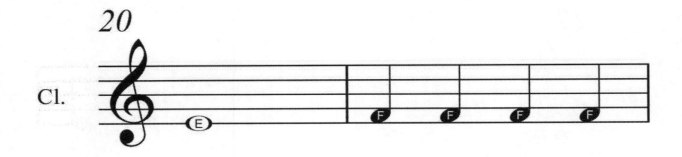

22
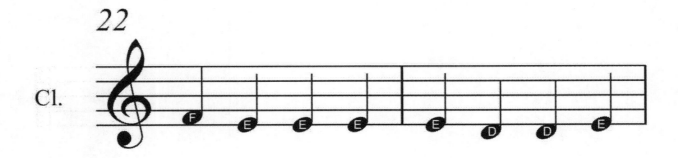

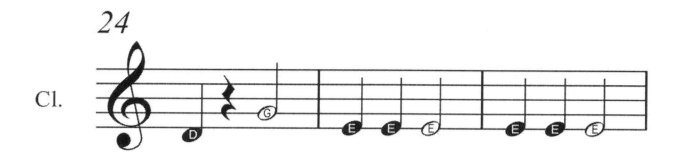
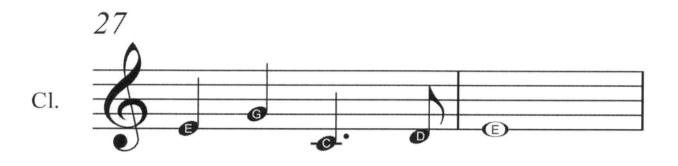
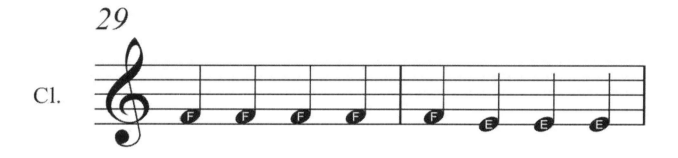
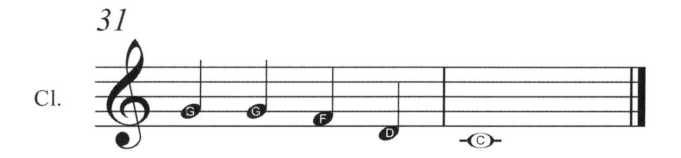

While Shepherds Watched Their Flocks

♩ = 100
Traditional

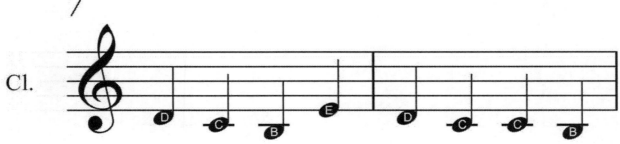

9

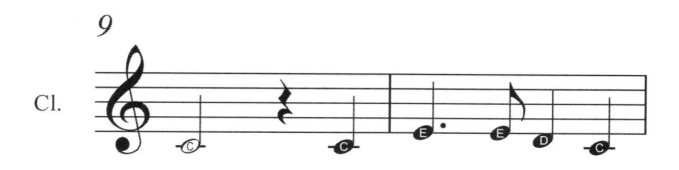

11

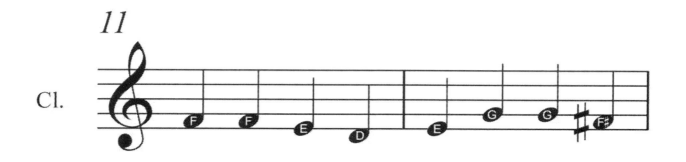

13

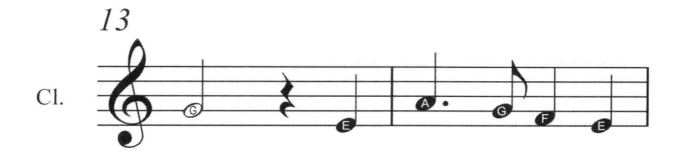

15

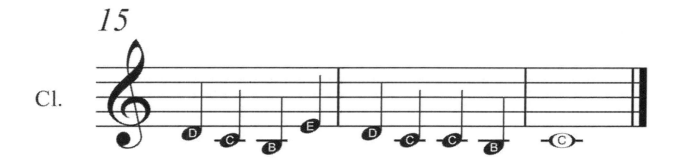

Good Christian Men Rejoice

Traditional

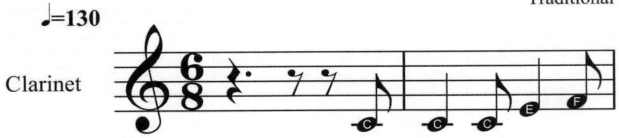

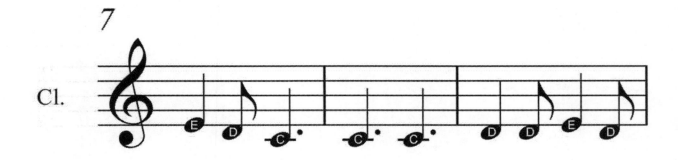

We Three Kings

John H. Hopkins

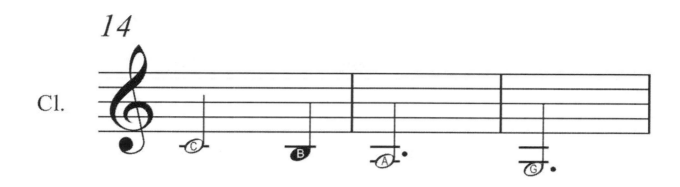

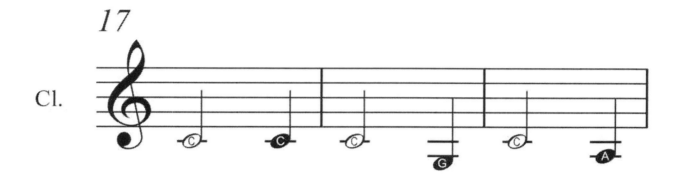

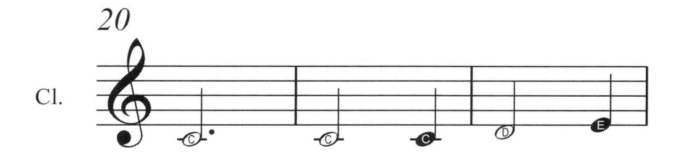

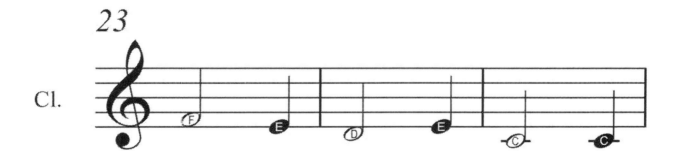

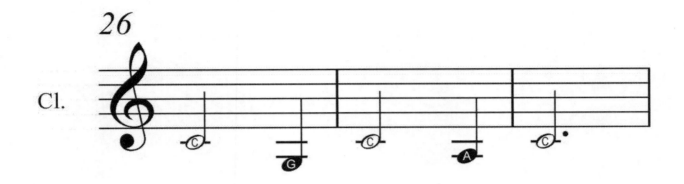

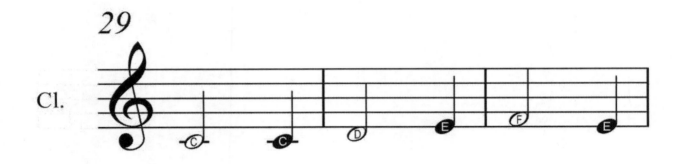

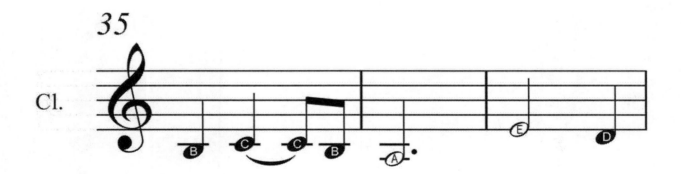

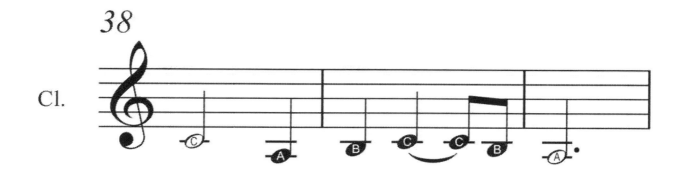
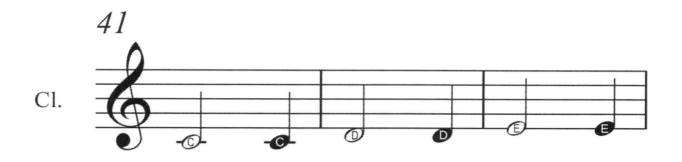
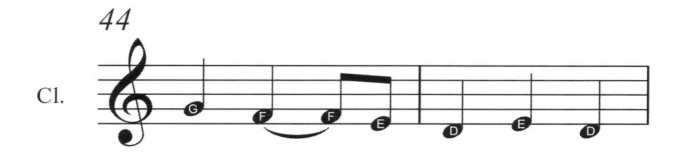
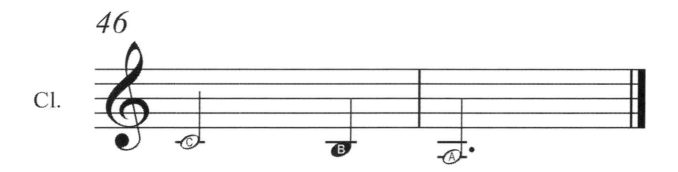

Angels We Have Heard On High

Traditional

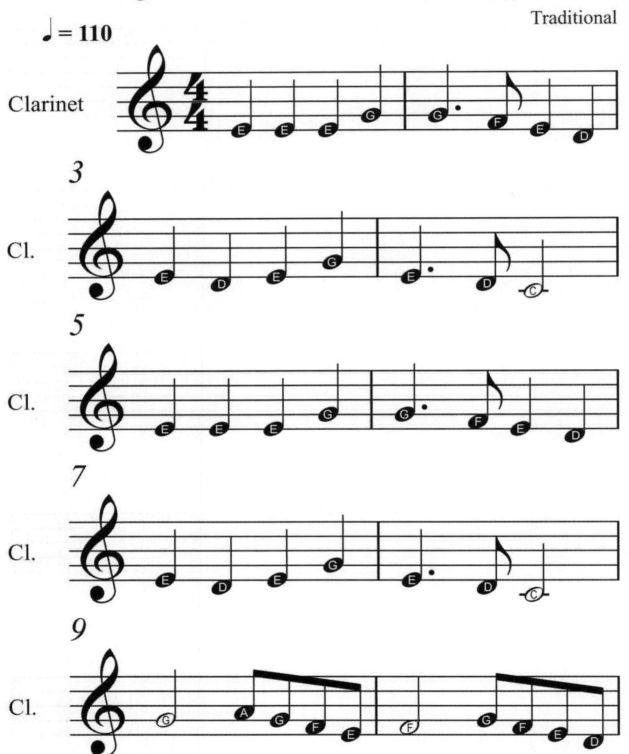

Go Tell It On The Mountain

Traditional

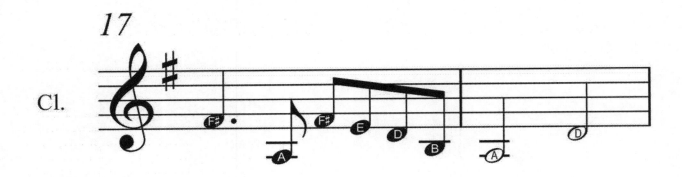
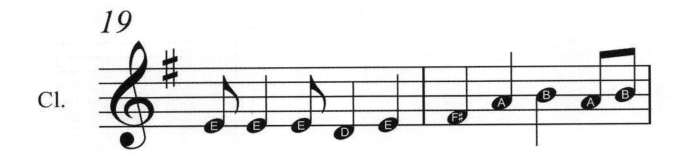
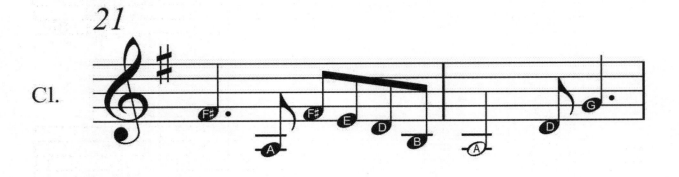

Angels From The Realms Of Glory

Henry Smart

It Came Upon The Midnight Clear

Traditional

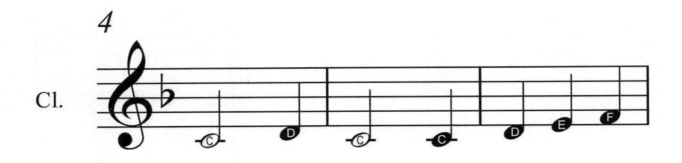

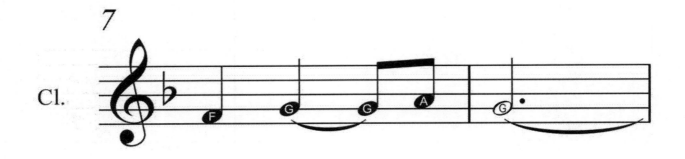

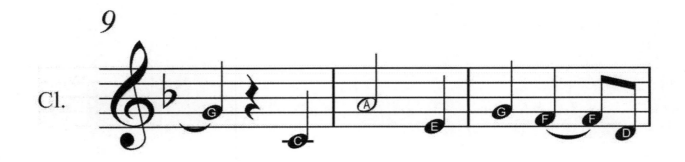

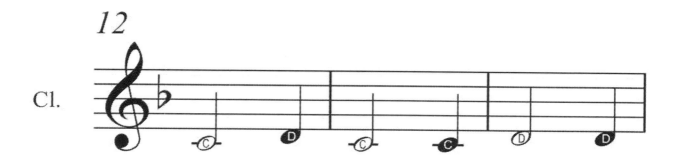

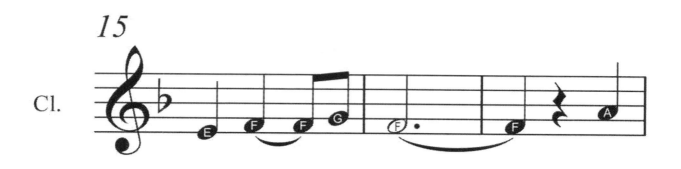

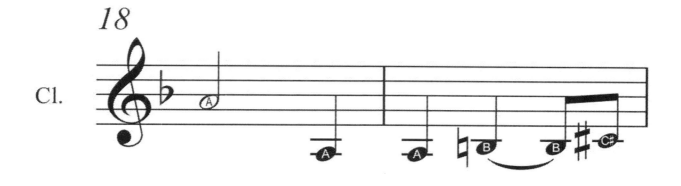

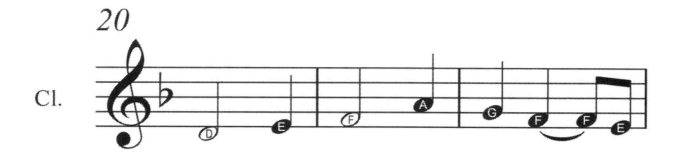

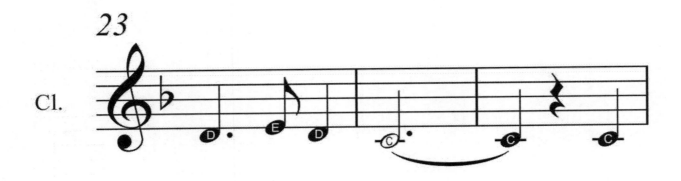
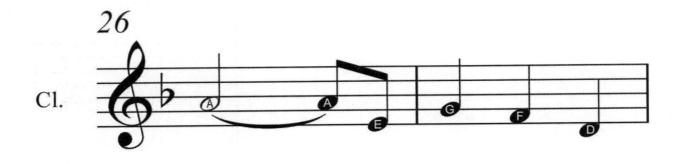
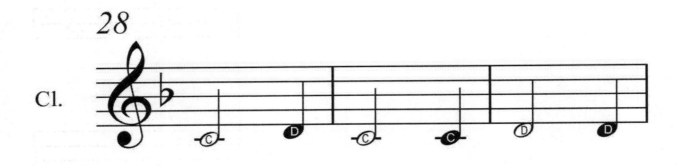
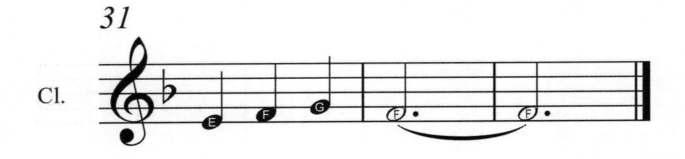

Coventry Carol

Traditional

31

Joy To The World

Lowell Mason

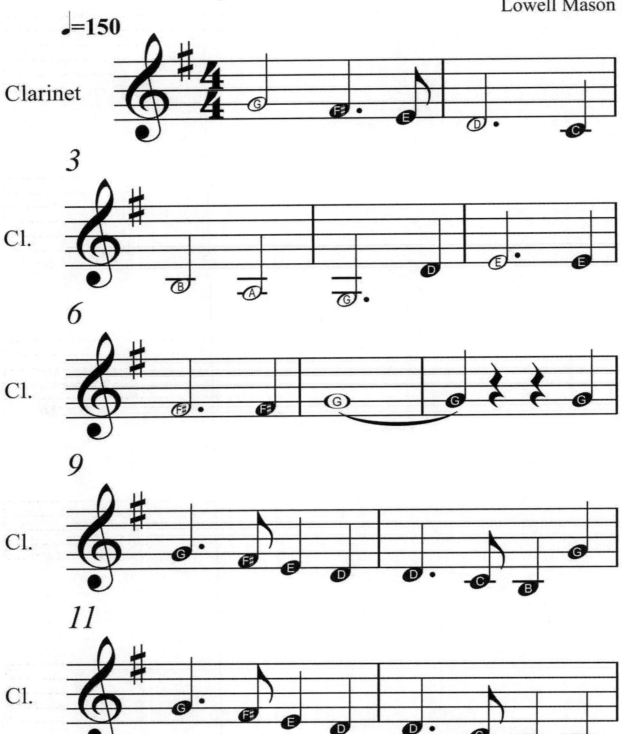

32

Christians Awake Salute The Happy Morn

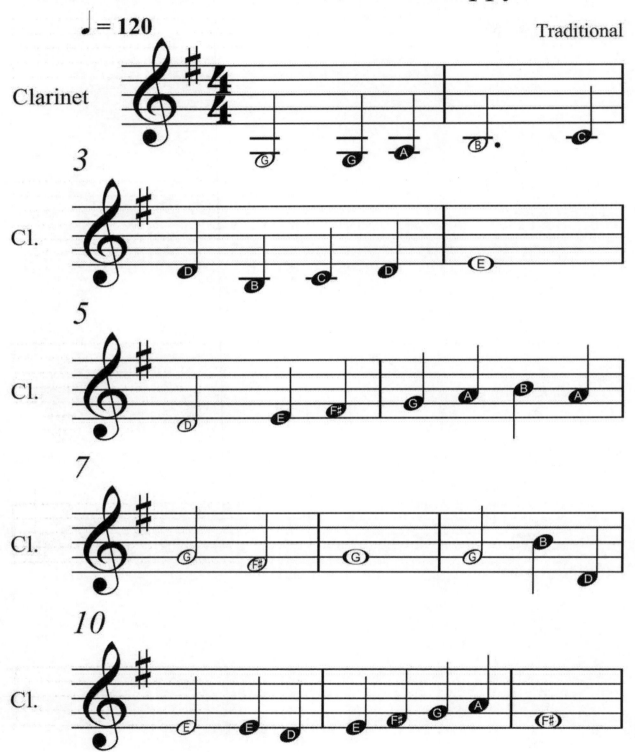

Good King Wenceslas

Traditional

♩ = 125

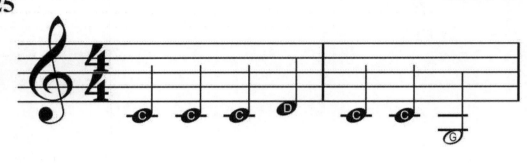

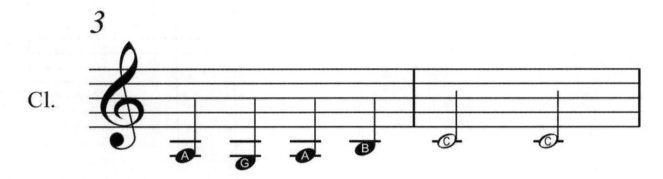

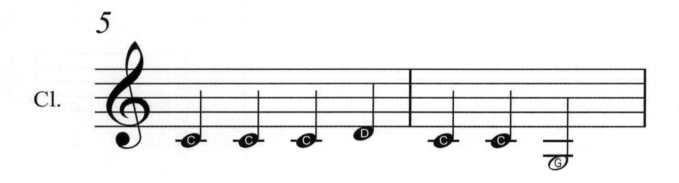

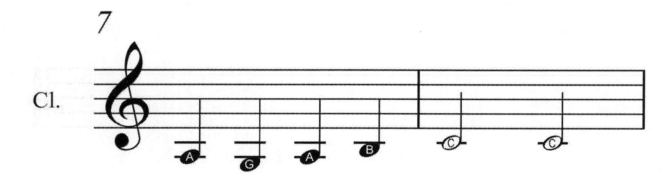

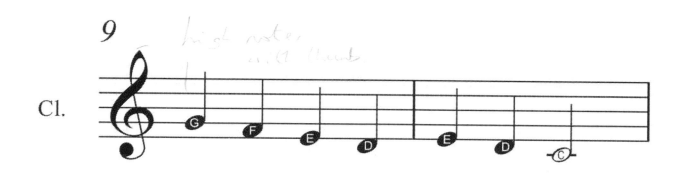
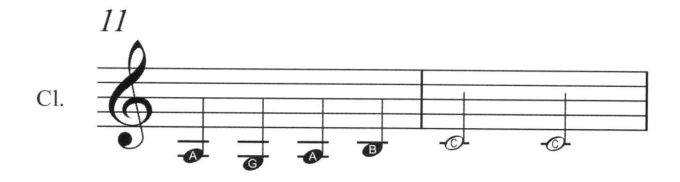
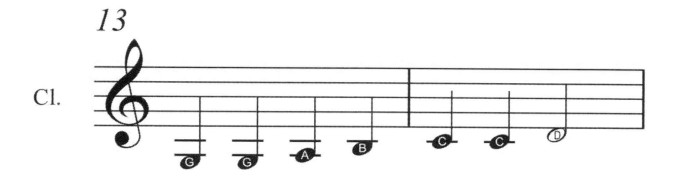
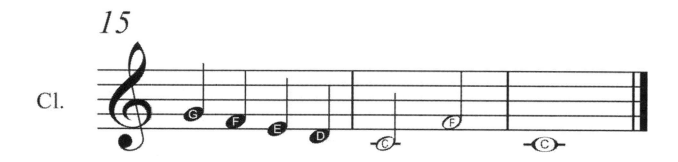

Come, All Ye Shepherds

Traditional

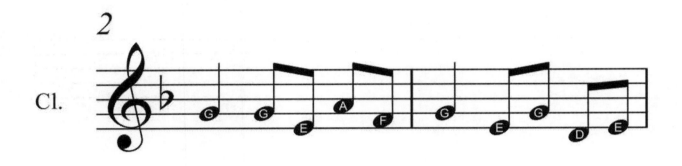
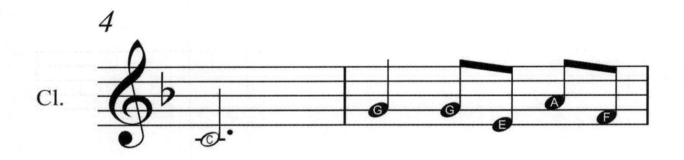
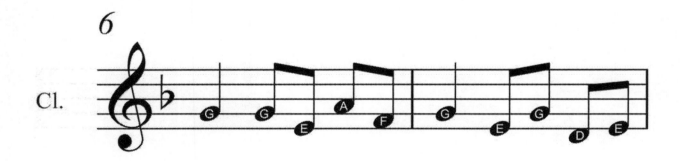

8

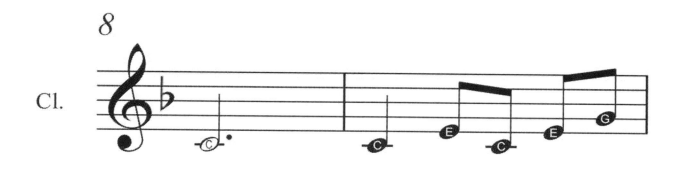

10

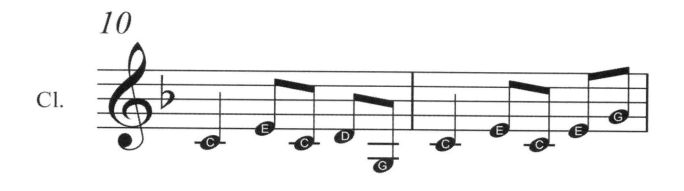

12

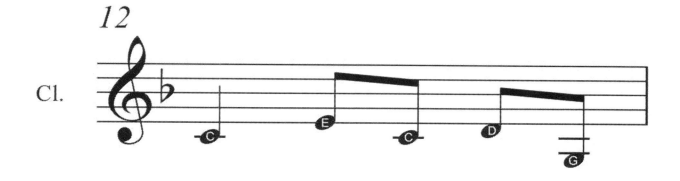

13

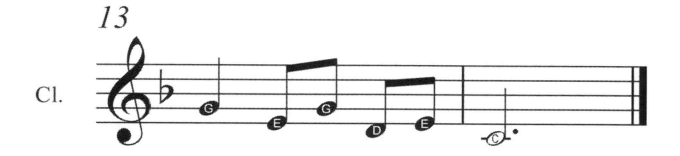

What Child Is This?

Traditional

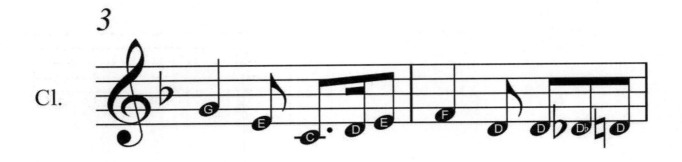

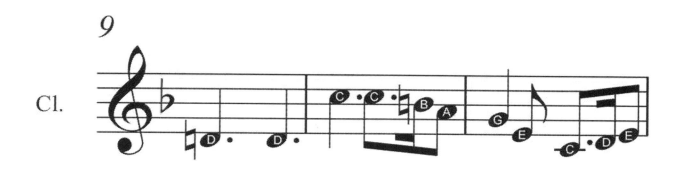

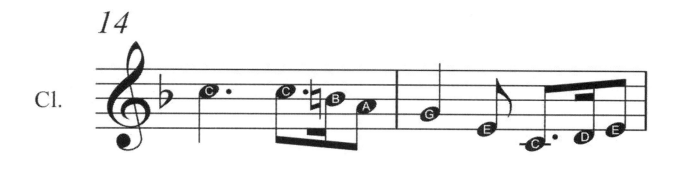

The Holly And The Ivy

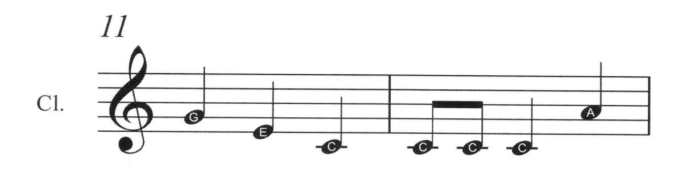

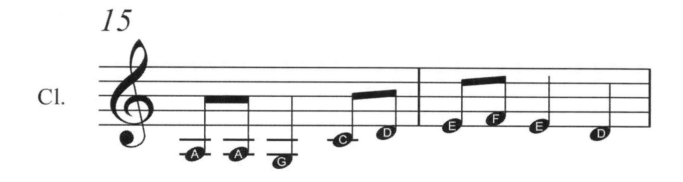

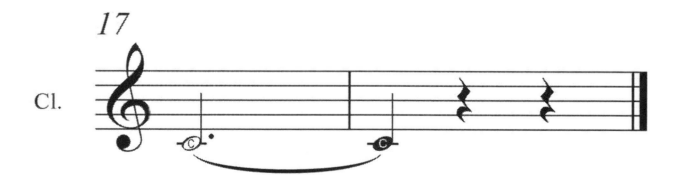

I Heard The Bells On Christmas Day

John Baptiste Calkin

About the Author

Mike works as a professional musician and keyboard music teacher. Mike has been teaching piano, electronic keyboard and electric organ for over thirty years and as a keyboard player worked in many night clubs and entertainment venues.

Mike has also branched out in to composing music and has written and recorded many new royalty free tracks which are used worldwide in TV, film and internet media applications. Mike is also proud of the fact that many of his students have gone on to be musicians, composers and teachers in their own right.

You can connect with Mike at:

Facebook
facebook.com/keyboardsheetmusic

Soundcloud
soundcloud.com/audiomichaeld

YouTube
youtube.com/user/pianolessonsguru

I hope this book has helped you with your music, if you have received value from it in any way, then please leave a review and encourage like minded musical instrument players around the world to keep playing music.

Thank You
Michael Shaw

Printed in Great Britain
by Amazon